Penguin Books
The Penguin Leunig

Michael Leunig contributes cartoons and
drawings to various papers and magazines,
including the Melbourne *Age*.
His work has appeared in *Woman's Day* and
London Oz.

The Penguin Leunig

CARTOONS BY MICHAEL LEUNIG

INTRODUCED BY BARRY HUMPHRIES

Penguin Books Ltd, Harmondsworth,
Middlesex, England
Penguin Books, 625 Madison Avenue,
New York, N.Y. 10022, U.S.A.
Penguin Books Australia Ltd, Ringwood
Victoria, Australia
Penguin Books Canada Ltd, 2801 John Street
Markham, Ontario, Canada
Penguin Books (N.Z.) Ltd, 182-190 Wairau Road,
Auckland 10, New Zealand

First published 1974
Reprinted 1974 (twice), 1975, 1976 (twice), 1977,
    1978, 1979, 1980
Copyright © Michael Leunig, 1974
Introduction copyright © Barry Humphries, 1974
Made and printed in Australia by
Alexander Bros Pty Ltd, Mentone, Victoria

Leunig, Michael.
    The Penguin Leunig.
    ISBN 0 14 004019 6
    1. Australian wit and humor, Pictorial.
    2. Caricature and cartoons—Australia. I. Title.
741.5'995

Introduction
by Barry Humphries

I once attended a dinner party given in my honour by a lady of taste and fashion. Over the avocado salad I chanced to mention that I had, that afternoon, recorded a television interview with a grinning member of Australia's omniscient Discjockocracy, and that our trivial exchanges were being transmitted at that very moment. In a trice my hostess and her friends evacuated the dining room to watch this grey, mind-numbing colloquy on the servants' T.V. set, and I spent the next thirty minutes alone toying with the debris of my meal, and pondering upon the alchemical properties of The Media. Could it be true that people and things and ideas and emotions were all somehow more exciting and glamorous and at once less inimical after they had been 'processed' by an electrical machine, isolated on a glass screen, and punctuated by advertisements for soap, cars and tobacco?

In this book Michael Leunig has illustrated the phenomenon. A simian family are watching a sunrise on telly, while behind them, out of the window, the Real Thing fulgorously happens. Do not suppose that I would have you compare my presence at a dinner party with dawn in the Blue Mountains, but Leunig's family of rapturous apes have much in common with my dutiful hostess and her friends. The ultimate compliment we can pay reality is to view its simulacrum.

Leunig has expressed the whole thing, with all its complexities ironies and absurdities, and with its pathos as well, in the simple and sublime form of a poetic joke. He is, of course, a poet, even more than he is a draughtsman or a droll. His jokes are all poetically conceived and that is why they touch the heart as surely as they make us laugh.

I first saw the work of this major Australian artist in the *Nation Review* a few years ago. Murky, melancholy and marvellous, his little *grisaille* paintings – for such they are – shone from the page amongst the writings of middlebrow radicals and flippant book reviews for with-it young marrieds. To be sure there were traces of influence from other artists whose work he may admire: Ungerer, Feiffer, Topor, Lear, Alfred Kubin, Arthur Boyd. Yet it is also possible that he has never heard of any of these but that his sensibility has, from time to time, overlapped their own, as often happens with artists of true originality and insight.

Leunig's subjects are as ambitious as his technique is simple. World cataclysm, The Flood, loneliness, cruelty, lust and greed. Through these runs the vein of his compassion and humanity – his humour – illuminating many a darkling theme. The persistence of the imagination in some insupportable urban setting. A man in a boat rows out of his apartment window towards a distant moon. His wife is concerned but shares his fantasy. 'You've forgotten your pond' she cries. There is the joke; there the Leunig poetry.

Sometimes whimsical, this prodigiously gifted artist is never guilty of whimsey, and, mercifully, he is never 'relevant', 'socially aware' or narrowly political. 'Social relevance' is a modish and peculiarly horrid little disease infecting modern criticism, invented by humourless puritans who are baffled by the magical uselessness of art. A claret-faced Melbourne hack recently reproached me for presenting a theatrical revue in which, so it seemed to him, I exhibited 'a sorry unawareness of how much life had changed'. Grub Street prigs expect jokes to somehow justify themselves by being 'satirical' or up-to-date: *relevant* in short. Interpretative artists – even vaudeville artistes – are not newsagents or telex machines thank God, yet they are suspect by drab minds if they fail to assert a 'point of view'.

Mr Leunig's 'point of view' may be seen by some who adore putting artists in pigeonholes as tragic and even misanthropic. To me he is too preoccupied with beauty and imagination to be thus narrowly assessed. In many of his drawings, the puny, often ludicrously painful antics of his human characters are witnessed by domestic animals and these he draws with the very greatest humour and compassion. Small dogs, and above all, ducks and geese, scamper around his comic tableaux like the creatures in Piero de Cosimo's paintings; they are the mute witnesses to human folly, vanity and loneliness. Mr Leunig's wonderful drawing of a man masturbating is comically moving, yet how much does the success of this drawing depend on the picture on the wall of this desolate room; a picture of duck! – a Leunig duck.

I hope this book will bring Leunig's art to the attention of a wide international audience. He deserves his country's honour because he is the only artist I know working for newspapers who seems to me to have a truly inspired comic gift. His geese may be bereft of social conscience, their cackling may not alert the Capitol, but if they awaken some of us to laughter they have not lived in vain.

Barry Humphries.

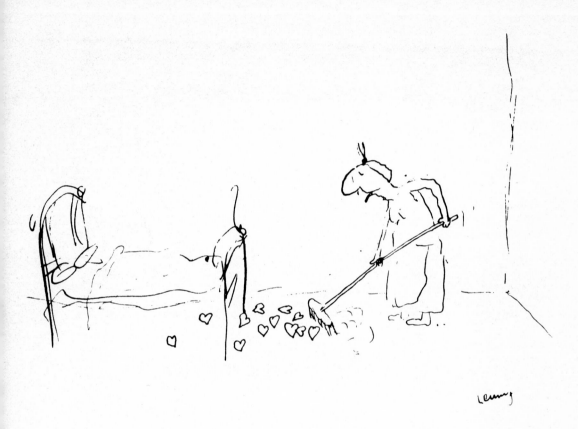

Jubilation at the Toucan Club when it is announced that the Korean war has ended.

STRICTLY NO WHEELING BABY NEPHEWS IN THE PARK

Leunig

"Waiter, there's a hair in my soup!"

Leunig

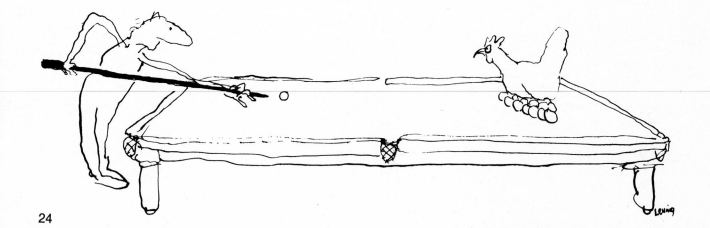

24

"Bulldust!"

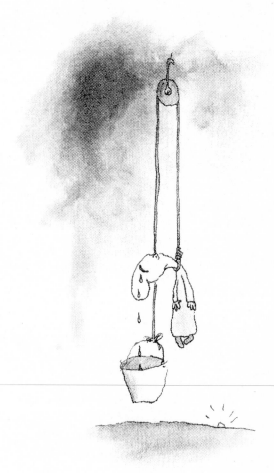

"Come on . . . play *The Golden Wedding again!*"

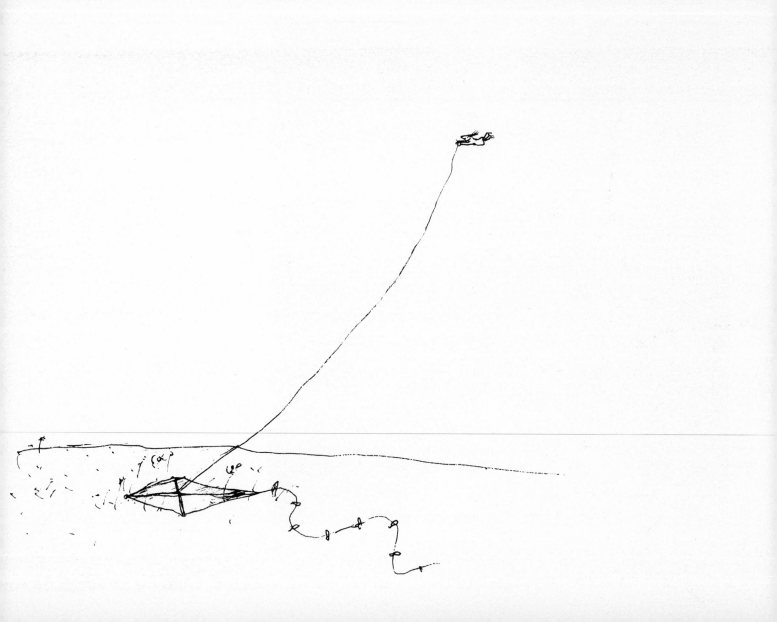

"Gee dad . . . you're fantastic!"

HEY HARRY...
WE'VE GOT
A PERVE
OVER
HERE

CLUB 31

"Hi ho, hi ho, it's off to work we go . . ."

The rare phenomenon of nude fog sucking . . . note thinness of fog around sucking nude.

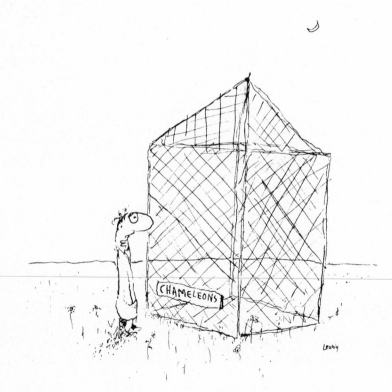

CHAMELEONS

Leunig

"Ahoy there!"

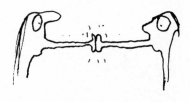

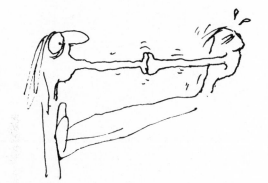

RRRIP

GI EE EYE
LITS ALK EASE

("GIVE ME MY
LIPS BACK PLEASE"
as spoken by a
lipless man.

Leunig

  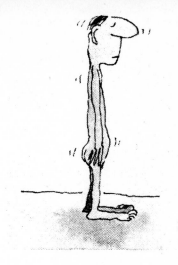

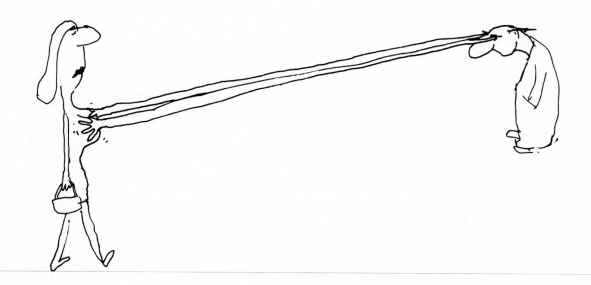

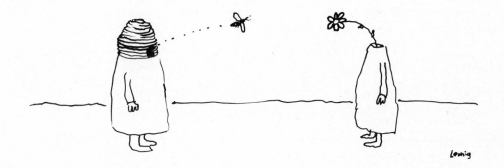

Male chauvinism or improvisation? — Sex object or agricultural implement?

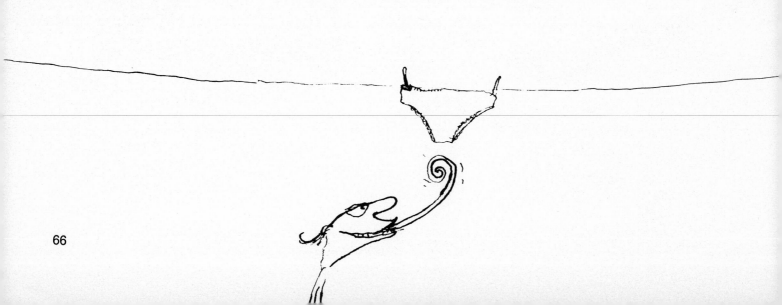

"Hoooooo . . . hoooooo . . . hoooooo . . ."

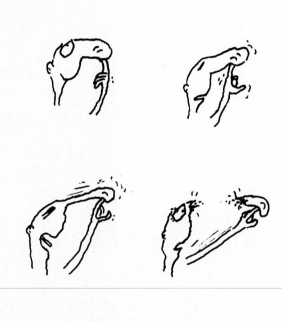

The Adoration of the Magpie

SITTING ON THE FENCE

Come sit down beside me
I said to myself,
And although it doesn't make
                    sense,
I held my own hand
As a small sign of trust
And together I sat on the
                    fence.

*"Of course they're upset . . . they were **expecting** a vision of the blessed virgin"*

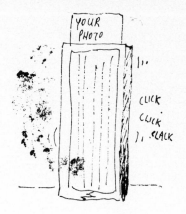

AN ORGANICALLY
GROWN tomato

FRIENDS
OF
THE
EARTH

Leunig

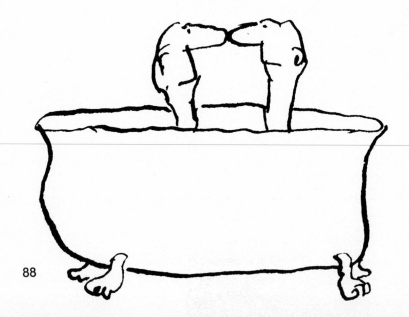

Leunig

OWED TO AUTUMN

I had a pair of trousers
A jolly shade of green
I wore them in the summertime,
And kept them bright and clean

Now autumn is upon us,
My pants are turning gold,
And soon they'll fall and blow away
To leave me bare and cold.

Leunig

Time bomb defusing . . . third year prac exam

Father, I'm confused.
One minute I'm up.....
the next minute
I'm down....

Then you must
pray to the patron
saint of ups
and downs....

ST. FRANCIS OF A SEE-SAW

Leung

"Hey stupid, you've forgotten your pond!"

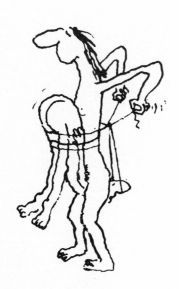

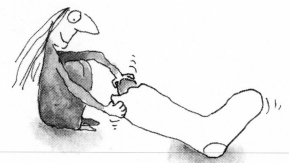

Leunig

A USEFUL HAIR MAGNET.

S.S. Whaler

SORRY

Leunig

111

113

"I dont suppose you'd have one without the dorsal fin . . .?"

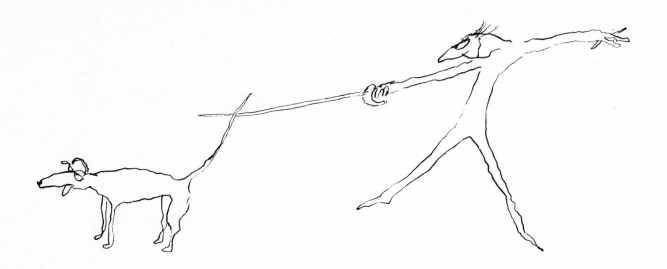

WELCOME TO HERE

When life goes by so quickly
That you feel you're just a blurr.
Then mumble vaguely to yourself.
Sort of, . "umm ... umm ..... errr..."

L.

Mr Curly comes home